OPTIONS TRADING

Basic Principles to Learn and Execute Options Trading Strategies to Get Started

WILLIAM RILEY

TABLE OF CONTENTS

Introduction

I want to thank you and congratulate you for downloading the book, *"Options Trading: Basic Principles to Learn and Execute Options Trading Strategies to Get Started."*

This book contains proven steps and strategies on how to make money and win in the options trading market by deploying the right tactics and making the right decisions in different market situations.

Options have a rich and deep history as trading instruments, and for people who have been in the stock market for a while, they are especially appealing as they belong to a class of instruments called derivatives. While they have some similarities to and dependencies on stocks, they actually have a huge separate ecosystem of their own. In this book, we will discover this very ecosystem and understand what it takes to do well in the options trading market.

In this step-by-step guide, you will learn what options are, how you can start trading them *right now*, what strategies you need to use in which situation, what market tips and tricks you need to be aware of, and what common mistakes you need to avoid in order to make great, smart trades on a consistent basis. We will also cover all the basic terminology so you never feel out of the loop throughout this book. Armed with these fundamentals, you will become a great options trader in no time! So without taking any more time, let's get started.

Thanks again for downloading this book, I hope you enjoy it!

Chapter 1

Getting Started

Options is a well-recognized term in the field of trading. Often people assume Options trading is a hard concept to grasp, but it is not so. With the right direction, Options trading can be a handy tool for investors. Bonds, Exchange-traded funds, mutual funds and stocks are some of the major classes that form the assets for investors. Another such asset class is Options. With the right handling and informed guidance, Options can prove to be useful even where other classes of assets fail.

As the name suggests, Options are a form of investment that provides us several options. Options can be purchased in the same way as other assets and thus also carry similar risks. It is well known that none of the investments are risk-free. It is suggested that the risks associated with Options are calculated before the trade is done.

Options are associated with derivatives. Derivatives are often paired with risky performance. In the words of Warren Buffett, derivatives are a weapon of mass destruction. The term "derivative" here refers to the derivation of the price of an object from another object. Options are also a form of derivatives under financial securities.

With correct knowledge of the working of options and proper usage of this knowledge in the market, one can steer the odds in their favor. There is no strict way in which options must be implemented; each investor can implement the options in the way they personally think would benefit them the most. Speculation can take a person a long way in the trading market. Even if an investor does not use options directly, they should still have some knowledge of the options as the company they might invest in might use these options. Options are a trending tool heavily implemented in MNCs.

Definition of Options

As discussed above, Options are a type of derivatives. The price of an option is determined by a subclass of asset or security. A straightforward definition of Options can be given as such: Options are agreements between a buyer and a seller in which the buyer has the right to buy a derived stock from a seller at a price determined previously within a given amount of time. Options are an alternative for those investors who do not wish to partake in investment at a high stake. With the help of options, such investors can buy and sell stocks. Speculation plays a huge role in the investments. An investor is willing to invest only when he speculates a hike in the stock prices before the agreement expires.

Options come with a variety of strategies associated with a spectrum of risks ranging from mild to severe. By practicing these strategies, we can create opportunities for unlimited profit.

What Makes Options Different From Stocks?

While in the traditional sense, options and stocks are very similar in concept although some major differences exist among them. These differences are as follows:

1. As mentioned above, Options are agreements and thus have an expiration period. This period may vary over weeks, months or a few years. This period depends on the type of options implemented.

2. Options are derivatives while stocks are not. The price of underlying assets of options is determined by the price of some other assets.

3. The values of stocks have to be strictly within specified numerical constraints while options do not have such constraints.

4. When it comes to stocks, risk is indirectly proportional to the stock prices. If there is a decrease in stock prices, the risk of loss is greater. However, it is not so in the case of options. Even if the stock prices drop, profits can still be earned depending on the strategy of the options implemented.

5. An investor who owns a significant portion of stocks in a company is given voting or decision-making rights, but it is not the case for options owners.

Things to Consider When Getting Started

Type of investors

The investor can be a company or an individual and options trading is significantly different for them in regards to regulations and legal proceedings. The investor should also know whether they could trade with offshore companies and bank accounts. They are beneficial when it comes to dealing with taxes imposed on trading.

Setting up an account

The basic step of getting started with options trading is to set up an online trading account first. It is an easy task and step-by-step tutorials are available for creating trading accounts, although the procedure can be lengthy, so it should be done at the earliest. The account setup is dependent on a number of factors which are explained below.

The amount of capital the investor can spare is a major factor in the setting up of an options trading account. For trading in stocks, a small amount of money can be invested, but for trading in options, a bigger sum of capital is required. There are three types of accounts out of which an optimal type can be chosen depending on the investor. They are:

- Day-trading account

- Regular account

- Margin account

A day-trading account allows unlimited buying and selling. A margin account allows the investor to access the earned money as soon as a sale is made and also allows borrowing of money while for a regular account, earnings can be accessed after a specific procedure following a sale and no money can be borrowed, the capital invested has to be the investor's own. A regular account is approved much quicker than a margin account so it is suggested that a regular account is set up before applying for a margin account as waiting for approval might halt the trade for margin accounts.

Brokers

A broker offers services such as providing the information regarding the trade and options. Brokers are easily available online and offline, but their service charges might differ. An investor should hire a broker depending on their investment and the margin of profit.

Research companies

Market conditions might change suddenly and unexpectedly and it is important for an investor to be up-to-date with the existing conditions of the market. The information they have is crucial for making investment decisions; therefore, the information should be exact and flawless. Research companies are such companies that research the market conditions and provide this information to the investors.

Benefits of Options Trade over Direct Assets

We have learned earlier that the risks associated with direct assets are huge and not all of these risks can be evaded. The profit of direct assets is directly affected by any change in the price of the asset.

In options trade, we have the option to implement a mixture of strategies in order to maximize the profit. Also, trade options are derivatives, which means the price of trade options is determined by the price of some underlying asset, but the investor is not forced to buy the asset. The investor has full right to practice his trading rights. Because of these aspects, trade options are considered a better alternative than direct assets as little investment can generate bigger profits.

The base of options trading is the agreement. This agreement allows the investor to buy shares of associated assets whenever they want. The number of option contracts is represented using contract multiplier. Trading options classes have unstable contract sizes. Say the contract size of options on some assets is 50, which indicates that the contract allows the investor to buy 50 shares from the seller. If the contract size is 100 and the price of 10 options is 10$ then the seller has to be paid 100$ and the buyer can thus buy 1000 shares. Consider a situation where the strike price is 40$. In this situation, the cost becomes 40x1000, which is 40000$. That is how a meager investment of 100$ has led up to an exposure of 40000$.

Options types

There are mainly two types of options:

Call option: Call options are used in regards to purchasing of the underlying assets. These assets have to be purchased before the expiration of the options contract. Upon practicing the call option, the investor gets the right to purchase the underlying assets at the strike price.

Put option: Put options are used in regards to the sale of underlying assets before the contract expires. An investor usually practices this option when they suspect a drop in the stock prices below the strike price.

Options Trading Terminology

Strike Price

The price at which an underlying asset can be bought or sold is called strike price. Strike prices or exercise prices are decided at the time of contract.

In reference to the call option, this price refers to the buying price of the underlying asset while in reference to the put option; this price refers to the selling price of the underlying asset.

Premium

As we know, options do not have a price of their own, they are derivatives which means the price of an option is determined by the price of their underlying assets. Premium is the sum of capital that has to be paid in order to buy an option. This sum is dependent on the market conditions, contract duration and price of underlying assets.

Underlying asset

Options are derivatives; their prices are determined by the price of underlying assets. These assets can be futures, currency, stocks, commodity, currency and such. In options trading, the stocks are these underlying assets. The option determines the prices and expiration of these stocks.

Option style

The options have an expiration date. Once the contract expires, the owner loses the rights to buy or purchase the underlying assets. This expiration date can be days, months or even years from the date of purchase. There are basically two popular options - European and American options. In the case of European options, the sale and purchase rights can only be practiced on the expiry date while in the case of American options; these rights can be practiced up to the expiration date. Thus, American options are more popular than European options.

Moneyness

The strategies of the options trading are realized using the moneyness of options. Moneyness is the term used to indicate the relationship between the current price of an underlying asset and the predetermined exercise price. These relationships are of three types namely ATM, ITM and OTM.

ATM: ATM or At The Money. This is the condition where the current price of the stock is equal to the strike price predetermined in the contract.

ITM: ITM or In The Money. ITM varies with the type of options. In the case of Call option, the strike price exceeds the current price of the underlying while in the case of Put option; the current stock price exceeds the strike price of the asset.

OTM: OTM or Out of The Money. In contrast to ITM, for call option, the current price of the underlying asset is higher than the strike price and for put option; the strike price exceeds the current stock price.

Intrinsic value

The price by which one type of price of the underlying asset exceeds the other type of price according to the ITM moneyness is known as intrinsic value. For example, if for the put option, the strike price of an option is 50$ and the current price of the stock is 35$, the intrinsic value is 15$.

Extrinsic value

For Out of the Money options, extrinsic value is the price that is calculated by subtracting the intrinsic value from the current price of the stock.

Exercise

Exercise is the action of the owner to sell and purchase an underlying asset. Exercise means practicing the owner rights.

Buy to open- sell to close

The options are purchased by deducting the cost from the trading account. Buying to open works differently for call and put options. For put option, use of the buying to open order means the trader will benefit from a decrease in the stock price and increase in the option price. For call option, the trader will benefit from an increase in the stock prices. Sell to close order is used after the buy to open order to close the previously used order.

Sell to open- buy to close

As opposed to buy to open order, sell to open order is used to sell an option and credit the thus acquired money to the trader's account. The call and put options for sell to open order works in the same way. To terminate a sell to open order i.e., to purchase the sold option back, the buy to close order is used.

What Makes Options Trading Attractive to Investors?

With options trading, the investor can earn big profits just by investing a small initial amount. This is possible because the owner of an option can choose to exercise their rights at any moment. A lot of speculation is required on the part of the investor. Also, the risks involved in options trading are less as compared to the direct assets trading. Despite all this, the understanding of options trading is sophisticated and requires good knowledge on the part of the investor.

Chapter 2

Strategies for Options Trading

The misconception about Options Trading is that it is very difficult to understand, but that is simply not the case. As we discussed in the above chapters, using options trading an investor can generate great amounts of profits from small initial investments with minimum risks. Options are powerful and flexible and can prove to be extremely beneficial if properly used. The way to do that is to gain knowledge about the working and fundamentals of options trading before starting the actual trade. We have also discussed that in options trading, we can combine various strategies to generate an optimized strategy to help us make the best out of options trading. Let us learn about these strategies in this chapter.

Covered Call

The covered call strategy generates profits through the means of premiums. There's a term called "Long" for covered call. This term is used to denote the purchase of assets with the optimism that the value of said asset would rise in the future. Selling call option on this long position enables the investors to generate recurring incomes. Covered calls are neutral in nature and it is estimated that for the duration of call option on an asset, the price of the asset will change only minutely, be it high or low. Covered calls are also known as buy-write. Although covered calls provide generous income on short terms, with some patience it can help the investors to generate income as a chain of premiums. If the investor is willing to wait out, they can choose to keep the underlying assets and not sell them even in the case of a small depression, elevation or inactivity, this works as a protection scheme on long asset position and generate income in premiums. A disadvantage is that if the price of the underlying stock exceeds the price of the option, then the investor has to give up the gains on stocks.

Covered call being a neutral strategy means it is not optimal for investors who are very brutish in terms of earning. It is suggested that such investors keep the stock on hold and not exercise the write option as if the asset price goes up; the option takes the profit on the asset. Also, if the stocks take a big hit and the estimated loss is going to be too great for recovery from premiums using the call option, the investor should sell the stocks.

Two terms are used for keeping track of profit and loss in this strategy, these terms are:

The maximum loss- It is calculated by removing the amount received as premium from the purchasing price of the underlying asset.

The maximum profit- it is calculated by calculating the total of strike price of short call option and premium received and then subtracting the purchasing price from it.

Married Put

Married put acts like a safety net in the field of options trading. The investor who is holding a long position has to purchase the at-the-money put option to prevent themselves from taking a big hit if the stock prices fall.

Married put is also known as synthetic long call. Some people may think married put to be similar to covered put, but that is not the case. Married put is optimal for those bullish investors who are wary of probable loss in near-sightedness. Another benefit of implementing the put option is that with this option, the investor gets to enjoy the benefits exclusively available to stockowners such as voting rights and receiving dividends. So is not the case if the investor has invested in a call only option. Same as the covered put, married put strategy can allow the investors to reap unlimited benefits generated from the initial investment in the underlying stocks. The only deductions from the profit will be the investment used for buying premium of the put option. There's a stage called breakeven at which the price of the underlying asset exceeds the price paid for the options premium. It is after this stage that the profit begins to generate.

Another new term called Floor is used, which is referred to the difference between the actual price at which the underlying stock was purchased, and the strike price of the put.

The exercise of a put options falls under the category of married put only when both the assets and the put option is purchased on the same day. The broker is then informed to deliver the bought stocks when the investor exercises their put option.

The question that now arises is when to use this strategy?

As mentioned in the first line of this concept, married put acts like a safety net or insurance for the investors and that is how it should be addressed, not as a money-reaping strategy. The price paid for purchasing premium of put is dedicated from the total profits. This strategy should be used to act as a protection of stocks for short terms so as to counter the probable dip in the stock prices. This gives the investor some sort of reassurance knowing that the chances of loss have been diminished and they can continue to trade.

Bull Call Spread

Bull Call Spread is ideal for use when a hike in the price of the underlying stock is estimated in the near future by the investor. In Bull Call Spread, the investor has to purchase two specific call options on the same underlying asset and within the month of contract expiration. These two call options are at-the-money call option and out-of-the-money call option. Upon beginning the trade, the Bull Call Spread takes a debit from their account, which is known as bull call debit spread.

The cost of implementing bullish options of the trade are eliminated by the sale of out-of-the-money call option.

The total profit is calculated by taking the difference between the strike price of the call options and the bull call debit that was taken at the beginning of the trade. Maximum gain is said to be reached when the price of the underlying assets exceeds the strike prices of the two calls.

Similarly, the maximum loss is calculated by the addition of all the costs incurred in the form of commissions and premiums. An investor faces maximum loss when the prices of the underlying assets fall near to the date of expiration and is either less than or equal to the higher strike price of the two calls.

A few terms are associated with Bull Call Spread, which are as follows:

- Break-even point: In the Bull Call Spread, The breakeven point is calculated by the addition of prices of the total premiums purchased and the strike price of the long call.

- Intense Bull Call Spread: Intense Bull Call Spread is determined by subtracting the lower strike price of two call options from the higher one. The investor can reap maximum profits only when the stock prices elevate by a significant margin.

What makes Bull Call Spread alluring to the traders?

There are a number of advantages of the Bull Call Spread strategy that attract the options traders. These advantages are-

A) There is a certain limit to the loss. Bull Call Spread prevents the investors from facing too huge losses.

B) Bull Call Spread generates higher returns from the initial investment than other strategies in which only call options are purchased.

C) More profits are generated when the price of the underlying assets do not rise above the price of the out-of-the-money short call option.

D) Call options can be bought at a lower price than the strike price.

What are the downsides of Bull Call Spread?

Since Bull Call spread generates more profits than the strategies in which only call options are bought, it means there are more purchases in this strategy than other strategies which means cost paid as the commission is higher. Bull Call Spread generates no profits if the price of the underlying asset exceeds the price of the out-of-the-money call option.

What additional steps can you take in Bull Call Spread to strengthen your position?

A) When the prices of the underlying assets are speculated to elevate above the strike price of the short call option, the investor can choose to implement the buy to close option on the out-of-the-money short call and then short it to again establish another out-of-the-money call. Another alternative to that is the investor may just exercise buy to close on the out-of-the-money short call option and leave it at that to reap benefits from the long call option.

B) In a situation where the prices of the underlying assets are not expected to change majorly, the investor can implement an out-of-the-money call option at a higher strike price, this transitions the Bull Call spread position to Long Call Ladder spread and the break-even point is decreased.

C) The investor can also transition into Bear Call Spread by closing the long call option. This is ideal for when the price of the underlying stock is speculated to turn back upon reaching the strike price of the short call. The transition has to be done as soon as the price of the underlying stocks becomes equal to the price of short call.

Bear Put Spread

This strategy is adopted in the situations where a drop in the price of the underlying asset is expected. Bear Put Spread consists of buying put options at a specific strike price and selling an equal number of puts at a lower strike price which share the same expiration date.

Two components make up the Bear Put Spread which are-

A) A short put having a low strike price.

B) A long put having a higher strike price.

Both of the puts share the same underlying assets and same expiration date. In the Bear Put, profits are achieved where there is a depression in the underlying stock prices.

These two components affect the profit and losses in these ways:

A) It limits the profits when the strike price of the short put having a lower strike price is higher than the price of the underlying stock.

B) It limits the loss when the strike price of the long put having a higher strike price is lower than that of the underlying stock.

Additions steps that can be taken for Bear Put Spread to strengthen your position

A) When the price of the underlying stock is expected to fall below the price of short put having a lower strike price, the investor is suggested to implement the buy to close the short put option and in return sell it to buy an out-of-the-money put option. Similar to Bull Call spread, the investor can opt for an alternative where he just implements buy to close on short put option and keep the long put as it is to reap the profits.

B) If a halt or a moderate drop is expected in the price of the underlying stock when it becomes equal to the price of the underlying stock, the investor can transition to Bull Put Spread by closing out of the Long Put option and purchase out-of-the-money put options.

What makes Bear Put Spread appealing to the investors?

There are a number of attractions that allure the investors. They are:

A) The most appealing feature of the Bear Put Spread is that it limits the risk of loss. This reassurance convinces the investors to try it out. The total amount paid for purchasing the put options in Bear Put Spread is lower than the price of a single put purchased independently because the capital spent for purchasing the long put option having higher strike price is compensated from the sale of the short put option having a lower strike price.

B) The price of shorting the assets is controlled by the cost of Bear Put Spread, which greatly reduces the risk. In case of a hike in the stock prices, the risk will become marginal in selling short stocks.

C) Bear Put Spread is commended to reap good profits when a depression in the price of the underlying stock from the date of the trade up to the date of expiration of the contract is speculated by the investors, but this fall in prices should not be too huge, as no additional benefits will be rewarded.

Drawbacks of the Bear Put Spread

A) The profit is limited if the price of the underlying assets goes lower than the price of the out-of-the-money options. No additional benefits will be rewarded.

B) The cost incurred in paying commissions is higher than the cost of outright purchasing single put options.

Protective Collar

Protective Collar is a strategy that is used for protecting the investment when the market becomes unstable and is susceptible to unexpected drops in stocks prices. Protective Collar provides downside protection that means it lowers the chances of losing the investment.

A Protective Collar consists of two components, which are:

A) Buying a put option to control the downside risk of underlying assets.

B) A call option is exercised to pay the capital to purchase the stocks. A covered call and long put position are joined together to perform this function.

It is through this pairing of the long put and short call option with their corresponding strike prices that this strategy acts as a protective Collar around the underlying stock. The two components share the same expiration date, purchased on the same underlying stock and are generally of the out-of-the-money options type.

To provide a collar of protection from the downside risk, we can work with the assumption that the strike price of the second component i.e., Call option exceeds the strike price of the first component i.e., put option. Let us understand this with an example.

Assume that the sale price of an asset is 60$, a put option with a strike price of $55 and a call option with a strike price of 65$ is purchased on this asset. This call option bought for $65 then serves as the protective Collar for the stock gains.

Optimal situations for implementing protective Collar

Protective Collar strategy is the most optimal for reducing the downside risks and at the same time not costing too much for providing this safety. This is done by exercising OTM calls on the protective puts, as puts are expensive to be purchased outright.

Limitations of Protective Collar

A single strategy cannot provide all kinds of benefits, and like each other strategy Protective Collar has its drawbacks too. The Protective Collar strategy puts the primary focus on the protection from downside risk while the upside is pretty much given up. It is optimal for as long as the strike price is falling, but as soon as the price starts rising the Protective Collar loses its appeal and all the profits beyond the strike price are wasted. In other words, it is good for the situations in which the price of the stocks start falling after rising continuously for a long time.

How does Protective Collar act as a hedge against Taxation?

As we have learned the major advantage of Protective Collar is its capability of providing protection from downside risks, but its advantages are not limited to only that, it has one another advantage.

Consider a case in which the price of the underlying stock is increasing at a rapid pace. Now the investor speculates two different scenarios, either the stock price will go even higher or the market will have a depression and the prices will fall. What would the investor do in that case? He/she has the option to sell the stock at the current price and wait for some time before purchasing it back and if the luck is on their side, they may even be able to purchase it at a strike price even lower than the price it was bought at before. But here's the catch, doing this may cause your profits to attract the taxes. The other major advantage of Protective Collar is that it saves your profits from this taxation by forming a hedge against the taxation by giving security against the drop in the market prices. Taxation will only be a problem if the investor decides to sell the stock and earn profits that way.

Long Straddle

The Long Straddle strategy generates profits from the shift in the price of the underlying asset, the shift can either be a decline or rise in the price, but it will only generate profits if it's marginal. The profit is generated when corresponding to the same underlying stock having the same expiration date, the investor purchases a long call and a long put on it. The profit generation possibilities are equal for the shift of the price of the underlying stock in either direction, though it is required that the shift manifested in the market should make the market go from a state of stability to instability.

The factors that cause this instability is usually something major such as something to do with elections, market laws, some government action or a major news. Bullishness and beariness are two reasons that form the instability in the market. Bullishness is when the market is under the threat of falling stock prices and beariness is when the market is speculated to face a rise in the stock prices. The beariness and bullishness counters each other to create instability in the market. However, the investors are not aware of the real cause of the instability and thus cannot determine whether it was the beariness or the bullishness. Long straddle is optimal in such conditions as in Long Straddle the profits are generated both from bullishness and beariness of the market. It still does not guarantee 100% profit as the market may not sway in the manner it is expected to.

It is a gambling game as the investor can only forecast and not be completely sure of the turn the prices of the underlying assets may take in the market. A new term introduced here is called Implied Volatility. Implied Volatility, as the name suggests is used to imply or predict volatility of the market in the near future and then accordingly pricing the options. A rise in the Implied Volatility while using Long Straddle strategy can generate profits, while a decrease in the Implied Volatility corresponds to a decrease in the value of the options.

To get rid of the risks resulting from the direction of the flow of Volatility in market, the investor can opt for buying both call and put options on the same underlying stock.

Calculation of losses and profits for Long Straddle

The alluring feature of the Long Straddle strategy is that the extent to which a risk can lead to losses is contained while the extent to which profits can be generated is unlimited. Such as, for when the price of an underlying asset hits rock bottom i.e., zero, the profit generated is given by subtracting the Premiums paid for the options from the strike price of underlying asset.

Consequently, the maximum risk is generated by the addition of the prices of the put and call options.

The formulas for calculating profits for rising prices and falling prices are given in the following ways:

- When the shift in the prices of the underlying assets in the market is upwards, the profit is calculated by subtracting the sum of the cost of premiums and the strike price of call option from the actual price of the underlying stock.

- When the shift in the prices of the underlying assets in the market is downwards or decreasing, the profit is calculated by subtracting the sum of the cost of premiums and the cost of the underlying stock from the strike price of the put option.

- The Maximum loss caused is given by the addition of all the commissions and premiums paid by the trader. Technically a loss is generated when the price of the underlying asset becomes equal to the strike price of the options.

Plus Points of Long Straddle

A) As we discussed above, the best and most unique feature of the Long Straddle is that it generates profits regardless of the direction of the shift in the market prices. There is equal potential for reaping benefits in both directions.

B) The market is influenced by a large number of factors such as news reports and federal laws. Knowing these can give us an idea of the direction of shift in the market prices.

C) The maximum loss in Long Straddle is not as drastic as it could be i.e., it limits the risk of the loss.

D) The potential of generating profits is limitless when the direction of the shift in the market prices remains same for a considerable amount of time.

Drawbacks of Long Straddle

A) Since profits are generated from the shift in the direction of the market prices, loss is generated when there is no shift in the prices of the underlying stocks.

B) When there is a drop in Volatility of the put and call options, loss occurs.

C) The cost of paying commissions by the traders is higher than direct purchase of options.

D) Loss also occurs if the current price of the underlying stocks becomes higher or lower than the strike price and does not touch any of the upper or lower break-even point.

Long Strangle

For the above strategies we have studied so far, all the call and put options were written on the same underlying stock having the same strike prices and the same expiration date, but the Long Strangle has a stark contrast in comparison to them. In the Long Strangle the underlying stocks and the expiration dates of both the put and call options remain the same, but their respective strike prices are different.

The principle of Long Strangle is similar to that of Long Straddle where profits are generated when there is a shift in the prices of the underlying assets, but the direction of the shift is not known or does not matter.

There are two types of strangles namely Long Strangle and Short Strangle.

The Long Strangle consists of two steps:

A) Purchasing an out-of-the-money put option.

B) Purchasing an out-of-the-money call option.

Both of the options are responsible for generating their share of the profits. The profit generation is distributed among both of the options in a way such that when the price of the underlying stock is continuously rising, the call option generates profits and when the price of the underlying stock is going down. Thus the potential for generating profits is unlimited.

In contrast to Long Strangle, the Short Strangle consists of the selling of both the call and put options previously purchased. Short Strangle does not offer unlimited profits and the maximum profit that can be generated is calculated by subtracting the cost of trading from the premium earned from shorting the two options.

A Long Strangle is made up of two major components that are a long put option having a lower strike price and a long call option having a higher strike price. The expiration date remains the same, but the strike price of the two components are different although they still are purchased on the same underlying stocks.

The potential of the profits when the prices of the underlying assets are rising is infinite as they can continue to keep rising without reaching a limit, although for the downward shift in the prices of the underlying stock, there is a limit to how low the stock prices can go which is zero, therefore profit potential is limited for falling prices.

The loss is generated when there is no shift in the prices of the underlying assets i.e., the market remains stagnant. If this remains the situation when the expiration date is reached and the stock prices remain equal to the strike price, loss occurs. The loss is calculated by the addition of all the capital paid for commissions and the premiums purchased by the traders.

The factor that causes this behavior of profit generation from the shift in the direction of the prices of the underlying stock is the Volatility of the market. The more volatile the market is, the more profits Long Strangle will generate. Profits occur when the price of the underlying stocks break through the upper or lower break-even points.

Long Call Butterfly Spread

Long Call Butterfly Spread differs from all the previous options strategies we have learned so far in the sense that the previous strategies only consisted of two components, but Long Call Butterfly Spread works with three. They're exercised in the following order-

A) Firstly the investor purchases a call option for a low strike price.

B) The investor sells two call options for a higher strike Rice.

C) The investor purchases another call having an even more expensive strike price.

The strike prices of all the call options written on the same underlying stock are different, but the expiration date remains the same. The potential profit in the case of Long Call Butterfly Spread is limited when the price of the underlying stock is found equal to the strike price of the short call on the date of expiration.

The maximum profit is calculated by subtracting the lowest strike prices from the in-between strike prices and then further subtracting the total cost incurred in terms of commissions and premiums and other things from the previous result.

The maximum risk occurs when at the day of expiration the strike price is either reaching past the highest strike price or the lowest strike price. Whichever constraint is breached, the maximum risk occurs. The maximum risk is calculated by the addition of all the costs incurred in realizing the Long Call Butterfly Spread position.

Speculating the state of the market

Long Call Butterfly Spread yearns maximum when the price of the underlying assets is the equivalent of the center strike price on expiration date, therefore, the state of the market is judged by how close or far the price of the underlying assets is from the center strike price. The forecast the market would either be neutral or there will be an expected increase in the market stock prices. The forecast is thus dependent on the center strike price in the following ways-

A) The forecast is said to be neutral when there is no change in the price of the underlying stocks. In Long Call Butterfly Spread, the forecast is neutral for the price of the underlying stock being equal or very close to the center strike price during the time of trade initiation.

B) The forecast changes to bearish when the price of the underlying asset is less than the center strike price during the time of the trade initiation.

Drawbacks of Long Call Butterfly Spread

A) Long Call Butterfly Spread is inferior from the Long Straddle and Long Strangle strategies in the sense that both the previous strategies had unlimited potential for profit generation, but Long Call Butterfly Spread has limited potential for profits.

B) Since there are more steps involved in the establishment of Long Call Butterfly Spread position, the cost of premiums and the commissions that the traders have to pay is also more than other strategies.

Iron Condor

When the market conditions are less volatile and the investor wants to implement a strategy with lower chances of risks, Iron Condor strategy is optimal. Iron Condor is famous among the veteran traders who have good experience with Options Trading. The word Condor is in reference to a bald large sized vulture, which resembles the profit/loss graph of the Iron Condor strategy.

The Iron Condor strategy combines the powers of two vertical spread strategies we studied previously namely Bear Call spread and Bull Call Spread. There are four contract options for these two vertical spreads with unequal values of strike prices while the expiration date remains the same for all.

Iron Condor position is established by selling and buying put and call options in the following manner where the investor has to first sell an out-of-the-money call and an out-of-the-money put option and at the same time buy an out-of-the-money call and an out-of-the-money put option.

The strategies we previously studied such as the Long Strangle and Long Straddle generate maximum profits when the market is in a volatile state and the prices of the underlying stock never seems to be stable. But what about when the market conditions are not volatile enough? Iron Condor is ideal for those situations when the price of the underlying stock is not expected to show much change as it can generate much more net profit as compared to other strategies in such a state.

It is important to note that the cost paid for commissions by the traders is high in the case of Iron Condor as there are 4 different option contracts.

Maximum profit potential is generated at the beginning of the Iron condor establishment. Profit is reaped as a result of less volatile state of the prices of the underlying assets in the market.

On the other hand, the maximum potential loss is calculated by the given formula-

Max potential loss = (Strike price of one spread - Strike price of another spread) x size of contract - Premium received

Plus points of Iron Condor

A) We have a way of calculating the maximum loss and profit potential prior to their occurrence.

B) Iron Condor is modifiable in the way that it can be transitioned into other strategies.

C) A transition can be made into the Bull Put Spread by closing out the call options when the price of the underlying stock rises and seems to continue for a considerable amount of time.

D) A transition can be made into the Bear Put Spread by closing out the call options when the price of the underlying stocks decreases and seems to continue for a considerable amount of time.

E) The net credit generated is much more than the net debit spent on the spread.

Limitations of Iron Condor

A) As it was mentioned earlier, the investors prefer Iron Condor with enough experience in the Options trading. It can be too complex for the investors who trade at lower levels.

B) The cost of the commissions is high because of the multiple number of call and put options.

Iron Butterfly

The strategy is known as Iron Butterfly because the shape of the profit/loss diagrams for this strategy resembles a Butterfly. There are two kinds of spreads for Iron Butterfly which are- Long Iron Butterfly Spread and Short Iron Butterfly Spread.

Long Iron Butterfly Spread

The Long Iron Butterfly Spread is made up of 4 components and requires the investors to purchase Bear put and Bull call spread. The strike prices of the Long put and Long Call are equal and share the same expiration date, but the distance between the strike prices is equal. In contrast to Iron Condor strategy, which was net credit oriented, Long Iron Butterfly Spread strategy is net debit oriented.

It shares more similarities with Iron Condor in the sense that the potential of profit is not unlimited, along with limited maximum risk. Also, the strategy is not ideal for uninformed traders as the strategy is quite complex in comparison to other strategies.

And since this strategy includes four different spreads and three different strike prices, the amount paid by the traders is also quite high which can only be compensated with timely and appropriate buying and selling of options.

Calculating maximum profit and losses for Long Iron Butterfly Spread

Maximum profit is calculated using this formula-

Profit = (Highest strike price - middle strike price - lowest strike price) - cost of the commissions and premiums paid by the trader

The profit is generated using different spreads in different scenarios in the following ways-

28

A) For the Bear put spread to achieve maximum profit, the prices of the underlying stock should remain less than even the lowest strike price when the expiration date arrives as a result of which the all the calls expire and the put options are still of in-the-money type.

B) For the Bull Call spread to achieve maximum profit, the prices of the underlying stock should be even greater than the highest strike prices when the expiration date arrives as a result of which all the calls expire and the call options are still of in-the-money type.

Maximum risk or maximum loss for Long Iron butterfly Spread can be calculated by combining the costs of all the debits incurred in the establishment of this position. This situation arises when the strike price of the underlying stock is the same as the center strike price of the long options such that when the date of expiration arrives, all the debits the trader paid for establishing the Long Iron Butterfly Spread are lost in the process and no profits are generated.

There are two break-even points in Long Iron Butterfly Spread, one known as the upper break-even point and the other one called lower break-even point. The upper break-even point is that point at which the stock price can be generated by calculating the sum of the net debit paid and the center strike price. The lower break-even point is that point at which the stock price can be generated by subtracting net debit paid from the center strike price.

Short Iron Butterfly Spread

The number of components in Short Iron Butterfly Spread remain the same as Long Iron Butterfly Spread. What actually changes is the type of bear spread and bull spread options. In the Long Iron Butterfly Spread where we purchased a Bull call and a Bear put spread, we now purchase a Bull Put and a Bear Call spread. The other aspects of the calling options remain same as Long Iron

Butterfly Spread which are- same expiration dates, equidistant from each other and also sharing the exact same strike prices.

The Short Iron Butterfly Spread differs from the Long Iron Butterfly Spread in the sense of orientation. While the former is net credit oriented, the later was studied to be net debit oriented. The risk/reward ratio of Short Iron Butterfly Spread is the same, as that of Long Iron Butterfly Spread and the complexity of the strategy also remains the same.

The calculation of maximum profit and risks also differ from the Long Iron Butterfly Spread. Here maximum profit is reaped at the condition that when the date of expiration arrives, the stock price is found equal to the strike price of the short options as a result of which the options expire generating no gain of their own. The actual calculation is done with the help of this formula-

Profit = Net credit - Cost paid by the traders in the form of commissions

Maximum loss occurs in Short Iron Butterfly Spread when the price of the underlying stock is beyond any of the highest or lowest strike price i.e., Stock price > Highest strike price or Lowest strike price > Stock price. It is calculated with the help of this simple formula-

Maximum loss = (Center strike price - Lower strike price) - Net credit

Maximum risk leads to two different scenarios:

A) For the Bull Put spread to achieve maximum loss, the prices of the underlying stock have to be less than even the lowest strike prices when the date of the expiration arrives as a result of which the call options expire and the put options are of in-the-money type.

B) For the Bear Call spread to achieve maximum loss, the prices of the underlying stock have to be higher than even the highest strike prices when the date of the expiration arrives as a result of which the put options expire, but the call options are of in-the-money type.

The break-even points of Short Iron Butterfly Spread are the same as we discussed above. The upper break-even point is reached when the price of the underlying stock can be calculated by the addition of center strike price and net credit. The lower break-even point is reached when the price of the underlying stock can be calculated by subtracting the net credits from the center strike price.

Chapter 3

Before You Enter a Trade

L et me stop you right there before you start making trades. There are a few things you need to be aware of before you enter the market. Let's read about them in this chapter so you can understand how to filter out the garbage and consistently pick good trades. Here are the steps you need to go through.

1. Portfolio Balance

Before you do anything, you need to look at your portfolio balance first. When you're planning a new trade, it's always important to ask yourself why you need that trade and how it will affect your portfolio. Do you even really need it? For instance, if your portfolio already has plenty of bearish trades, it would generally be better for you to avoid adding more.

You need to reduce your risk in every situation, so the key here is to balance out your trades. That's how one develops a great portfolio, risk diversification. When you have a bunch of bearish trades in hand, look for bullish trades to offset the risk and vice versa. Once you internalize this, it becomes far easier to focus on what your portfolio really needs and filter out the rest from the very first moment you start looking for a new trade.

2. Liquidity

Liquidity is straight up one of the most important qualities of a good, tradable option. You don't want to be stuck with an illiquid option, no matter how lucrative it looks. Here's a simple rule to follow when looking for a new trade: for it to be a good trade, the underlying stock should be trading at least 100,000 shares daily. If the numbers are less than that, the trade isn't worth your time. In a market as big and efficient as the one we have, the calculations only become more accurate with the passage of time. Similarly, when considering the underlying options, there should be a minimum of 1000 open interest contracts for the strikes you are trading for it to be a good trade. It ensures quick entry into and exit from the market. Remember, liquidity is important!

3. Implied Volatility Percentile

When a trade satisfies the previous two criteria, it's time to move on to the next step - the IV percentile. You need to check relatively how high or low the implied volatility of an option is, and this is measured by using percentile scores. Let me explain with an example.

Say, if AAPL has IV of 35% but IV percentile of 70%, it means that while the current volatility is low, in the last one year, it was higher than what it currently is (35%) for more than 70% of the time. So the implied volatility for AAPL is *relatively high*, and you should be looking to employ *premium-selling strategies*.

4. Picking a Strategy

Picking a great strategy is as much a matter of eliminating as it is a matter of selecting, perhaps even more so. You can easily eliminate a bunch of strategies once you have a good idea of the IV and the IV percentile of the underlying stock and how it affects the options. For example, it's easy to eliminate strategies like debit spreads and long single options when you know the IV is high and the pricing rich. Then it's time to consider our risk tolerance and account size to pick the best strategy out of the ones left (iron condors, credit spreads, strangles, etc.).

5. Strikes & Month

Your personal trading style and goals also play a big part in how you decide to pick trades. Some people are more risk-averse than others, and that's okay. You should always select the right strategy based on the risk level you're comfortable with. If you're selling credit spreads, let's say, and you have the option to sell them at either a strike price that has a 90% chance of success of a strike price that has a 65% chance of success, you need to decide which option you wanna go with based on the level of aggression you're comfortable with. It needs to fit your trading style and your goals. Another thing that you need to do is give yourself sufficient time. This makes sure the trade can work out. This means that you should place low IV strategies at 60 to 90 days out and high IV strategies at 30 to 60 days out. To understand why this is the case, you should read up on Theta value (one of the Greeks) and how it affects volatility.

6. Position Size

Position sizing is one of those areas where even some of the more experienced traders fail. It's crucial that you understand this concept so you can make great trades often. Before placing a trade, you should always carefully assess your position size. As your trading position gets bigger, so does the risk, but this isn't linear, as many studies have shown. The risk increases exponentially, and one bad trade could easily lead to a blown account in this case. I strongly advise you to start with small positions as a beginner and continue to do so even when you're an intermediate. Your risk scale should be a sliding scale of 1 to 5% of your total balance on which all your trades need to be placed.

Now, how does one define this risk? Let me explain.

The cash or margin you use to cover a trade is what we call risk. For example, when selling a $1 wide credit put spread for 50 cents, you would need to cover it up with $50 margin. You use this $50 margin to base your trade off of for each trade you make. If your account is worth $20,000 and you wish to allocate 3% of your account (it fits the 1-5% sliding scale criteria), you can take $600 of risk (3% of $20,000). Then you divide this by $50 and you get 12, which is the number of spreads you should sell at most. If this number is a fraction, always round down and never up.

7. Future Moves

You must've heard the popular saying that a chess grandmaster can foresee as many as 20 moves ahead. A good options trader also plans ahead and foresees future moves. If you're not thinking a few moves ahead, you're going to lose to the market more often than not. Always have a Plan B in case things go nasty and you need to shield yourself from losses. And while shielding yourself from a losing trade is important, it's also important to plan how to turn a losing situation into a winning one.

Sometimes, you just won't be able to make a winning trade. That's just how the market works; some trades go wrong no matter how well you plan. But you need to keep asking yourself the important questions constantly. When you do this, your mind stays sharp and ready to jump into action to formulate a new plan or make an adjustment as and when the need arises.

Chapter 4

More about Options Strategies

In this chapter, I will tell you about some additional tips and tricks you should be aware of in order to be a better trader.

Be Aware of This before Jumping into the Trading Business

The success rate in Options trading is basically dependent on the type of strategies the investor adopts. Various strategies can be combined together to produce maximum profit for the investor depending on the different states of market conditions and the investors themselves. The market conditions refer to the volatility of the market or the stillness of the stock prices. There are different types of investors such as the patient investors who are willing to wait to generate more profits, or investors who want to reap profits as soon as they invest. The goals of these strategies is to maximize the profit potential and minimize the losses. A new investor should always start with the basic strategies. Simple basic strategies are used to generate more complex strategies suitable for all kinds of conditions and with time and information, investors become more experienced and capable of handling complex strategies.

The information and implementation of all the basic strategies with their corresponding plus points and limitations have been explained in the previous chapter.

Learn from Others Mistakes

Earning in the stock market is not an easy task. People often find themselves losing their investment because of the unexpected turn in the market conditions and sometimes because of their own mistakes. Now, an investor cannot be aware of all the possible mistakes, but some of these mistakes are very common and this knowledge can be used to prevent them from happening. Given below is a brief description of some of the common mistakes that investors make in Options Trading.

The Price Tag Problem

Deep out-of-the-money options are very cheap compared to other options and the profit is generated for these options when the market is volatile i.e., the changes are quick and marginal. Now the newly entered investors are vary of spending a lot of money so they purchase these cheap and deep out-of-the-money options and if by apparent luck they do earn profits, they get confident about these options but too much volatility in the market is not usually long-lived and when that Volatility vanishes, the risk of loss becomes too high.

Greed and Fear of the Investors

Greed is a big part of human nature and when it comes to money, it overpowers other emotions. Since trade has a huge potential for making profits, greed is hard to give up. It is this greed that leads investors to lose their patience and make unfavorable decisions. Similarly, fear is something every human experience in their life and the fear of losing their investments causes the investors to be on edge all the time, which may again lead to unfavorable results. This is why it is of utmost importance that the investor keeps these emotions in check when making trading decisions to avoid risks and loss.

Recovering the Losses

Stocks trading and options trading are quite different in practical applications because their prices depend on different factors. Some of the strategies that work wonders in the case of stocks trading may plunge you deep into losses in the case of options trading.

It is often heard that some people invest a lot in the options trade in the hope of recovering from any past losses. But instead of recovering bit by bit, they may want to recover all of the losses at once which is a very appealing thought in theory, but in practical life, the risk of losing is so high it may cause them to lose even more than before. Therefore it is suggested that recovery from loss is made in smaller steps to reduce the risks.

Shorting

Shorting a stock refers to buying a stock and then selling it immediately in the hope of purchasing it back again at a cheaper price in order to earn extra profits. Now the question that arises is when to buy back the shorted stock back? Markets are quickly changing, a delay in the buying back of shorts may cost you a lower price than the current price or it can cause you to lose your initial gain. But it is important to remember that a little profit is still better than any loss. Therefore it is suggested that the investor does not wait too long before buying back the shorts. Even if he can preserve a smaller percentage of the initial profit, it is better than losing it all if there is a big risk involved.

Various Risks and How to Avoid Them

The risk potential is the extent to which the losses can occur. It is important for an investor to know the risks involved in their investments and the strategy they are employing to manage their options trade. They should be aware of the limitations of their plans.

An investment should be made if the risk involved is not too serious and can be overcome with intelligent planning. There are various risks that occur in the market. These are expiration date, volatility of the market and lack of protection schemes against the risks.

With expiration date coming near, the risk of loss becomes greater if the price of the underlying stocks expires at zero. The expiration date should always be kept in mind while establishing and closing positions.

Volatility of the market is the quick movements in the stock prices in the market. This movement can either be upside or downside or both happening in random order. The investor should be aware of the implied volatility.

It in unwise to sell options without securing them. Various protection schemes should be implemented to avoid the chances of limitless losses.

Chapter 5

How to Excel in Options Trading

There are a couple things each investor should remember when exercising options trading. Let us teach you what these things are.

Movement of Market

The major focus of the inexperienced investors is on the falling and rising of underlying assets prices. But simply implementing strategies for generating profit from upside and downside movement of the market is just not enough as these strategies fail if the movement stops or becomes insignificant. Sometimes the market is not volatile and the shift in the prices of the underlying stocks is so less it does not even matter. Call options are dependent on the rising of prices or generation of profits while the out-of-the-money options lose all of the investments if there is no rise in the stock prices. Therefore it is really important to think upon the strategies you are implementing and the state of the market before starting the trade. The market conditions may not always be as favorable in the short run as they are in the long run and as a consequence of this, long-term options are costlier.

Stock Charts

A stock chart is a plotting of various attributes of the stocks on a chart; these attributes are majorly prices and the timeframe. It is important for an investor to read up on stock charts according to the options they're planning to buy. There are stock charts for different timeframes such as one month, three months or even the whole year. Reading the charts informs the investors about how the prices are moving in a market within a specified timeframe. The rise and fall of the stock prices can be easily noticed from these charts and this information can be used to create a plan for the investment and options trading. It is not enough to see just the one-month chart as the prices in the chart may seem to be stable, but that may not really be the reality. Sometimes the movement in prices is quite slow and can only be actually noticed over a longer timeframe. From the recent changes in the prices of the underlying stock, an investor can speculate the future movement of the prices. The speculation may not always be up to the mark as a few other factors can shake up the market unexpectedly.

Move with the Trends

An investor can determine the ongoing trends in the market by studying the stock charts. Usually, when a market is following a trend for a considerable amount of time, it is expected that it will continue to do so. Using this speculation, the investors try to make money off these trends. Going against the trends in some situations can be fruitful, but it is rare and usually betting against the trends causes the occurrence of losses. Trends are seldom interrupted in the short term and it is not easy to beat them, therefore, a newcomer trader is suggested to move with the trends.

Limiting the Losses

Losing in the options trading market is nothing new. Everyone loses once a while, but what actually matters is how much you've lost and if there is a way to limit this loss. Assume a trader has a well thought out plan for earning big profits, but due to some reason his plan fails and he is starting to lose. Now the ideal thing for the investor to do should be limiting the loss at the earliest. Losing a percentage of your total investment is still better than losing all of your investment, therefore, it is important for an investor to know when to pull back and sell their position to minimize the losses.

Option Chain

Option chains are a listing of all the call and put options that can be purchased for a given underlying stock. These different types of options are further separated in the list in different columns. Not only the types, but the strike prices and expiration dates of the options are also mentioned in this list. There is another attribute call volume of the contracts, which is a statistic of how often a specific control is traded. Repeatedly traded contracts have a higher volume and the contracts that have never been traded or traded really rarely have volume zero. Investors are often suggested to go with the contracts having a higher volume as more trades indirectly points to more chances of success in their previous exercises. Similarly, options with higher strike price and long expiration period are recommended for the investors. Purchasing options with less volume of these attributes is full of risks and is not recommended for inexperienced traders. The market is also considered to be more volatile during the opening and closing hours of the day. The shift in the activity with the time of the day should also be noted by the traders.

Cut your Losses

Learning to cut losses is one of the most important lessons you can learn as a new trader because it's usually one of the hardest things to learn. Cutting your losses takes courage; it takes rational thought. Humans really don't like to admit when they're wrong, so accepting the fact that you've messed up and the losing trade you're betting on will only worsen with time takes a lot of courage. When things go wrong and your predictions don't pan out, limit your losses and do it quickly. The longer you dally, the further the stock moves. You might end up losing all your money.

A good rule of thumb? Never let your losses go beyond 50% on any of your positions. If you purchased an option for $6 and the price is down to $3 after a few days, it's best to sell it and recover what you can. Waiting around any longer would most probably result in losing even the remaining $3. Cut your losses!

Cash is King

The trading tip "Cash is king" is applicable in more than just one context, and that is why it's so valuable. It also builds up on our last tip about cutting your losses.

Basically, "cash is king" simply tells you to deal with any difficult situation by separating your emotions from it. Say, you're expecting a stock to move up, but it doesn't. It's reasonable to get anxious in this situation and have second thoughts about your plans. That's when you separate your emotions from the situation by taking the cash off the table.

How do you do this? You take half your money and cash it out by selling your position, leaving the other half on the table to give it more time. The biggest benefit of this is the peace of mind, which should certainly not be underestimated. At the end of the day, you will be much less stressed about your position and much more capable of enjoying a good night's sleep. And secondly, you will be protecting yourself against huge losses while also ensuring you don't completely miss out on big profits.

Conclusion

Thank you again for downloading this book!

I hope this book was able to help you to understand the fundamentals of Options Trading. We have covered a variety of topics like the various strategies used in options trading, how to implement them well, and how to avoid common mistakes in order to make consistent profits in the market. I hope you take your time to understand all these concepts and do some more reading on advanced topics.

The next step is to get started on using the knowledge you've gained through this book. Set up your trading account and start putting the strategies to use. Be patient with yourself and remember to manage your risk well. I wish you the best of luck!

Finally, if you enjoyed this book, then I'd like to ask you for a favor. Would you be kind enough to leave a review for this book on Amazon? It'd be greatly appreciated!

Thank you and good luck!

References

https://www.investopedia.com/options-basics-tutorial-4583012

https://www.thebalance.com/options-definition-3305952

https://investinganswers.com/dictionary/o/option

www.ingramcontent.com/pod-product-compliance
Lightning Source LLC
Chambersburg PA
CBHW072257170526
45158CB00003BA/1095